Just Be

Moving Beyond

A JOURNAL INTO SELF-DISCOVERY

Dr. Chris Bjorndal

www.firstchoicebooks.ca
Victoria, BC

Note for Librarians: A cataloguing record for this book is available from Library and Archives Canada at www.collectionscanada.ca/amicus/index-e.html

Cover and layout design by Jenny Engwer, First Choice Books

ISBN: 978-1-77084-624-1

Printed in Canada ♻ on recycled paper

 FIRST CHOICE BOOKS

firstchoicebooks.ca
Victoria, BC

10 9 8 7 6 5 4 3 2

To the writer,

The art of writing in my journal has been a saving grace to me for over 40 years. I often ask patients to journal and not everyone is open to the idea. It is my hope that you will be.

For me, journaling serves many purposes:

- It is a safe place that I can unload all that is weighing on my heart, mind, body and soul

- It is where I write my poems

- It is a trusted friend that I can always turn to for advice, wisdom and guidance

- It is a memory box to record my life's events – the good, the bad, the ugly and the precious

- It is a place where I can process difficult emotions without any judgments

- It is a creative outlet for my writing

- It is an amazing sleep aide

There is no right or wrong way to journal. One suggestion is to practice stream-of-consciousness writing: just let the pen flow and see what comes out without any concern about rereading it later. When I do this kind of writing it is often illegible, but it comes straight from the heart without over-thinking. This allows me to get into a state of flow.

Another style of writing you can use is akin to record keeping: detailing events, feelings and thoughts in order to reflect on it later. This helps you to identify patterns of thought and behaviour from a wider perspective. For this style you might have to write a bit neater!

You may also find expression in rhyming lines, sketching, asking yourself questions and leaving space for a later answer or any other style you feel will help give a voice to what's inside *you*. I have included quotes for reflection – I encourage you to reflect on them, to think about what the words mean to you. I hope they resonate with you.

The act of writing – putting pen to paper – is a dying art, a dwindling practice displaced by technology. As you use this journal, take a moment to feel the paper in your hands, to listen to the sound of your pen gliding across the page and to appreciate the gift of language as your words fill the pages. If you need help getting started, use the quotes as a guide, allowing the words to gently nudge your soul forward as you reflect on their meaning for you.

My hope is that the physical, mental, emotional and spiritual aspects of yourself will receive the best medicine as you fill these pages. I wish you relaxation, comfort, solace, compassion and wisdom.

Sending you healing thoughts,

Dr. Chris

_____

_____

_____

_____

_____

_____

_____

_____

_____

_____

_____

_____

_____

_____

_____

_____

_____

_____

_____

"Are you creating *calm* in the way you are responding to
your life, or are you contributing to *chaos*?"

— DR. CHRIS

"Life shrinks or expands in proportion
to one's *Courage*"

— ANAIS NIN

_____

_____

_____

_____

_____

_____

_____

_____

_____

_____

_____

_____

_____

_____

_____

_____

_____

_____

"The happiness of your life depends on the
quality of your thoughts"

— MARCUS AURELIUS

"Between the stimulus and response there is a space. And in that space lies your *power* and your *freedom*"

— VIKTOR FRANKL

"Mistakes are part of the dues one pays for a full life"

— SOPHIA LOREN

_____

_____

_____

_____

_____

_____

_____

_____

_____

_____

_____

_____

_____

_____

_____

_____

_____

_____

_____

"Are you thinking about the *past*
or worrying about the *future*?

Remember to ask yourself where you are living in your
mind because you only have the *present moment.*"

— DR. CHRIS

_____

_____

_____

_____

_____

_____

_____

_____

_____

_____

_____

_____

_____

_____

_____

_____

_____

_____

"Remember to *rest* in the midst of resistance.
Lean into your breath and *relax*"

— DR. CHRIS

"Do you have the *patience*
to wait until the mud settles and remain
unmoving until the right action arises by itself?"

— LAO TZU

_____

_____

_____

_____

_____

_____

_____

_____

_____

_____

_____

_____

_____

_____

_____

_____

_____

_____

_____

_____

"When you are stuck, what are the *thoughts* you are believing? Do you need them?"

— DR. CHRIS

_____

_____

_____

_____

_____

_____

_____

_____

_____

_____

_____

_____

_____

_____

_____

_____

_____

_____

_____

_____

_____

_____

"You grow up the day you have your first
real *laugh at yourself*"

— ETHEL BARRYMORE

"Remember *you* are going to be with you the longest. It is vital you get the relationship right with *yourself* first before seeking love from another"

— DR. CHRIS

"Most of the time when we are *blocked* in an area of our life it is because we feel *safer* that way"

— JULIA CAMERON

_____

_____

_____

_____

_____

_____

_____

_____

_____

_____

_____

_____

_____

_____

_____

_____

_____

_____

_____

_____

_____

_____

"Vulnerability is the cornerstone of confidence"

— BRENÉ BROWN

"If we had not *winter*, the spring would not be so pleasant;
if we did not sometimes taste *adversity*,
prosperity would not be so welcome"

— ANNE BRADSTREET

"Happiness must be *cultivated*.

It is like character. It is not a thing to be safely left alone for a moment, or it will run to weeds"

— ELIZABETH STUART PHELPS WARD

"The heart of the *soul* is where beauty lies"

— DR. MICHAEL MASON-WOOD

"A moment of *self-compassion* can change your day.
A string of such moments
can change the course of your life"

– CHRISTOPHER GERMER

_____

_____

_____

_____

_____

_____

_____

_____

_____

_____

_____

_____

_____

_____

_____

_____

_____

_____

_____

_____

_____

_____

_____

"The goal is to move from self-improvement or self-judgment to *self-acceptance* and *self-love*"

— DR. CHRIS

"Peace is the result of retraining your mind
to process life *as it is*
rather than as you think it should be"

— DR. WAYNE DYER

"In order to *heal it*, you need to *reveal it*"

— DR. CHRIS

"Make peace with the present moment
piece by piece"

— DR. CHRIS

"New beginnings are often disguised as painful endings"

— LAO TZU

_____

_____

_____

_____

_____

_____

_____

_____

_____

_____

_____

_____

_____

_____

_____

_____

_____

_____

"There are many roads to *wellness*.
The important thing is to pick a path
and to follow it *wholeheartedly*"

— DR. CHRIS

"*Life* is important. Make sure you aren't sacrificing *today* for tomorrow"

— DR. CHRIS

_____

_____

_____

_____

_____

_____

_____

_____

_____

_____

_____

_____

_____

_____

_____

_____

_____

"Often the moment when we most need to *pause*
is when it feels most intolerable to do so"

— TARA BRACH

_____

_____

_____

_____

_____

_____

_____

_____

_____

_____

_____

_____

_____

_____

_____

_____

_____

_____

_____

_____

_____

_____

"Give yourself the gift of health and invest in your most
important asset – *you*!"

— DR. CHRIS

"If you want others to be happy, practice *Compassion*.
If you want to be happy yourself, practice *Compassion*"

— DALAI LAMA

"Every given moment we have two options:
to step forward into *growth* or to step back into *safety*"

— ABRAHAM MASLOW

"I cannot give you the formula for success, but I can give you the formula for failure – which is: Try to please *everybody*"

– HERBERT BAYARD SWOPE

"The only limits you have are the limits you *believe*"

— DR. WAYNE DYER

"Hardships often prepare ordinary people for
an *extraordinary* destiny"

– C.S. LEWIS

"Ultimately, the goal is to learn to *respond* from a place of emotional calm, like a still lake, versus *reacting* with disruptive emotional waves like a lake in stormy weather"

— DR. CHRIS

_____

_____

_____

_____

_____

_____

_____

_____

_____

_____

_____

_____

_____

_____

_____

_____

_____

_____

_____

_____

_____

"The *environment* of the cell
determines the *health* of the cell"

—DR. CHRIS

_____

_____

_____

_____

_____

_____

_____

_____

_____

_____

_____

_____

_____

_____

_____

_____

_____

_____

_____

_____

_____

_____

"*Happiness* is not found in what you possess, but in what you have the courage to *release*"

— NATHANIEL HAWTHORNE

_____

_____

_____

_____

_____

_____

_____

_____

_____

_____

_____

_____

_____

_____

_____

_____

_____

_____

_____

_____

_____

_____

_____

"If you want to be happy, *be*."

— LEO TOLSTOY

"I have learned that *loving* and *accepting* myself
is the respite from my mind that my soul needs"

— DR. CHRIS

_____

_____

_____

_____

_____

_____

_____

_____

_____

_____

_____

_____

_____

_____

_____

_____

_____

_____

"With awareness of faulty beliefs
in the *present moment,*
we can change our future behaviour"

— DR. CHRIS

_____

_____

_____

_____

_____

_____

_____

_____

_____

_____

_____

_____

_____

_____

_____

_____

_____

_____

_____

_____

_____

"Do you *love yourself* enough to make the changes
that you need to make?"

— DR. CHRIS

_____

_____

_____

_____

_____

_____

_____

_____

_____

_____

_____

_____

_____

_____

_____

_____

_____

_____

_____

_____

"To *be yourself* in a world that is constantly
trying to make you something else is
the greatest accomplishment"

— RALPH WALDO EMERSON

"Imperfections are not inadequacies.
They are *reminders* that we're all in this *together*"

— BRENÉ BROWN

_____

_____

_____

_____

_____

_____

_____

_____

_____

_____

_____

_____

_____

_____

_____

_____

_____

_____

_____

_____

_____

"Are you *accepting* yourself or *excepting* yourself?"

— DR. CHRIS

~ 82 ~

_____

_____

_____

_____

_____

_____

_____

_____

_____

_____

_____

_____

_____

_____

_____

_____

_____

_____

_____

"The world is round and the place which may seem like
the *end* may also be the *beginning*"

—IVY BAKER PRIEST

"Are you *connecting* with yourself and others
or *contracting* from yourself and others?"

— DR. CHRIS

"There is *no quick-fix* solution
to multi-factorial conditions"

— DR. CHRIS

"Not until we are *lost* do we begin to
find ourselves"

— HENRY DAVID THOREAU

"In order to heal the *mind* you must first heal the *heart*"

— DR. CHRIS

Dr. Chris is a mom, wife, daughter, sister and friend. She is a Doctor of Naturopathic Medicine in Edmonton, Alberta with a focus on the treatment of mental health concerns, eating disorders, women's health and fertility. A speaker and author, she has shared her personal story and philosophy of wellness with audiences across North America.

She has helped many patients navigate through labels and stigma towards mental, emotional, physical and spiritual wellbeing. She loves her work and balances it with a full, active lifestyle with her husband and son.

To learn more about Dr. Chris and authors of quotes in this book, see:

Dr. Chris . . . . www.drchrisbjorndal.com

Tara Brach . . . . www.tarabrach.com

Dr. Wayne Dyer . . . . www.drwaynedyer.com

Brené Brown . . . . www.brenebrown.com

Christopher Germer . . . . www.mindfulselfcompassion.org